The 47s

Compiled by
Howard Johnston

Copyright © Jane's Publishing Company Limited 1987

First published in the United Kingdom in 1987 by
Jane's Publishing Company Limited
238 City Road, London EC1V 2PU

ISBN 0 7106 0450 5

Printed in the United Kingdom
by Netherwood Dalton & Co Ltd, Huddersfield

JANE'S TRANSPORT PRESS

Cover illustrations

Front: During the Indian summer of Edinburgh-Dundee
locomotive-hauled services, ScotRail Executive-liveried 47637
passes Burntisland on 19 September 1986 with the 0930 Dundee-
Edinburgh. *(Peter J Robinson)*
Pentax 6 × 7 150mm Takumar Ektachrome 200 1/500, f6.3

Rear: Full yellow cab fronts grace D1871 (now 47221), seen at
Kirkham & Wesham with a Whit Monday Sheffield-Blackpool
excursion on 29 May 1967. *(Barrie Walker)*
Leica M2 Kodachrome II

This page: No 47573 *The London Standard* passes Postwick, between
Brundall and Norwich, on the 1406 Great Yarmouth-Liverpool
Street on 28 June 1986. This loco was new to Tinsley in October
1964 as D1768, renumbered to 47173 in 1974 and conveniently to
47573 eight years later after eth conversion at Crewe. It was named
The London Standard with non-standard plates at Liverpool Street
on 9 June 1986, and was the first to receive an NSE repaint.
(Michael J Collins)
Olympus OM1 100mm Zuiko Kodachrome 64 1/500, f5

Introduction

It seemed a good idea at the time to build a vast standardised fleet of Type 4 diesels to become the backbone of BR's passenger and freight fleet. After all, conformity meant fewer problems.

So much for the theory of the 1960s. When problems did start to emerge with the Brush Type 4s, Class 47s, call them what you will, BR couldn't do much but make the best of a mediocre job. After all, you can't replace a fleet of 512 locos overnight. You simply undertake a progressive series of modifications to get a workable solution. A quarter of a century later, and a full replacement design is in sight. That means the writing is on the wall for a type that has become a sight virtually anywhere in Britain there is a railway.

To enthusiasts still recovering from the loss of steam traction, the Class 47 epitomised everything that was dull and monotonous about BR in the "corporate image" days. The smart two-tone green livery they carried from new lost its gloss, and the application of seemingly gallons of high-visibility yellow paint to their front ends rendered any visual design merits utterly redundant. From the 1970s, blue livery was marginally worse.

Thanks go therefore to Stratford for breaking the mould. It was the first depot to use initiative first in liveries and then nameplates. Others followed suit, BR liked what it saw, and the result ten years later is a veritable rainbow of hues that make the Class 47s a much sought-after commodity with rekindled enthusiasm by colour photographers. The pleasure of Class 47 photography is that you never know what will turn up next. No 47500 *Great Western* is just as likely to appear on the Edinburgh-Carstairs shuttle or at Aberdeen as 47640 *University of Strathclyde* is at the buffer stops at Milford Haven.

A technical work this book isn't, but the captions are intended to explain what has happened to each machine as it has gone through a series of conversion, renumbering and most recently renaming processes. First it was D1500-1999 and D1100-11, now it is 47001-901, with an increasing number of gaps of course.

The country's most skilled photographers are sharing some of their finest moments with us — our thanks go to them.

HOWARD JOHNSTON
Huntingdon
January 1987

Right: A classic pose of an ex-works Brush Type 4 — D1574 is only hours out of the Crewe Works paint shop on 18 April 1964, and yet to turn a wheel under its own power. Comparing this colour scheme with later daubings, it may be considered that only with the present InterCity and large logo paint styles have BR found schemes to match the beauty of the original two-tone sage and olive green, perfectly complemented by an integral half yellow warning panel and red buffer beam. D1574 was soon at work as a Gateshead loco, and renumbered 47454 has most recently been part of the Crewe fleet. *(Colin Ding)* *Rolleiflex   80mm Planar High Speed Ektachrome 1/500, f8*

Left: The doyen of the 512 Class 47s, 47401 is caught in pristine condition at Gateshead depot on 16 December 1981, groomed for its naming there as *North Eastern* two days later. Assembled at the Brush Works at Loughborough in 1962 with components originally ordered for a further series of Class 46 "Peaks", D1500 as it then was ran widespread trials on the Eastern and Western Regions before settling into a thoroughly conventional lifestyle. While many of its early design sisters were condemned during 1986, 47401 managed to slip through for one last overhaul. The National Railway Museum used to speak of its preservation, but will it keep its word? *(Peter J Robinson)* *Pentax 6 × 7 Ektachrome 200   2 sec, f11*

Above: The maroon-liveried coaching stock is a memory, but 20 years after this view of Shrewsbury was taken, the loco still covers the same trackwork. It is D1610, and the train is a Paddington-Birkenhead through service. As will be seen in following pictures, the two-tone green livery so smart in this March 1967 view did not wear too well. D1610, built for Cardiff Canton in August 1964, is still a Western Region loco, having passed through the steam-heat renumbering phase as 47031 to become electric-heat 47560, and acquire the name *Tamar* at a ceremony at Laira depot open day on 25 April 1982, ironically to be transferred away to Landore only a couple of weeks later. *(Barrie Walker)*
Leica M2   Kodachrome II

Right: A pre-electric scene at Kings Cross on 20 September 1971, and a shabby still-green Class 47 1761 coasts past the signalbox with the stock for an early-afternoon Peterborough semi-fast service. (Who, by the way, would recognise this loco nowadays as Old Oak Common's 47611 *Thames?*) The safety people have already got their way, and the stylish Class 47s became downright ugly box-like objects after an almost indescriminate application of yellow paint that lacked real thought. The end of steam on 4 August 1968 meant the end of the D-prefix, which was often painted out at depots in the opposite shade of green! 1761, at that time a Finsbury Park loco, started life at Tinsley, and moved across to the WR in March 1975 as 47166. Freshly fitted with eth equipment it was the second 47 to get the *Thames* nameplates after 47511 went to Scotland for push-pull work. *(Colin Ding)*
Rolleiflex   80mm Planar
High Speed Ektachrome   1/500, f5.6

Above: Frodsham Junction, linking the Birkenhead Joint (Great Western and LNW) and LNW main lines, is still there, and so is this loco, D1839, albeit in the guise of blue-liveried 47189. Never far travelled, D1839 was delivered from Brush's Loughborough Works in April 1965, and has been an LMR loco for its entire career. Built new with dual-brake equipment, it has only recently had its Stone Vapor steam-heat boiler declared redundant. Date of picture, 1 June 1967. *(John Feild)*
Yashica JP   Agfa CT18   1/250, f5.6

Left: A long train of short-wheelbase vans is now virtually unknown on BR, but was a common sight on 6 November 1965 when D1682, the first Brush Type 4 allocated to the Western Region at the end of 1963 (and also the first to the LMR), passed Tyseley. The 47s were being turned out in vast numbers by this time, and this loco, now 47096, was also the first of the second Brush batch, following D1549 off the production line. *(Michael Mensing)*
Nikkorex   50mm Nikkor
Agfa CT18   1/500, f2.8

Chinley North, former junction for the Peak Forest route to St Pancras, on 13 June 1973, and D-less Class 47 No 1950, still in green livery, heads west with a train of oil tanks from Sheffield. One of the later Brush products of September 1966, this loco should by rights have been turned out new in blue. Renumbered to 47259 under the TOPS configuration soon after this shot was taken, it was converted to electric heat the following year and renumbered again to 47552. Its longevity was further assured at the end of 1986 when it was provided with extra fuel tank capacity as part of a special fleet of 20 allocated to Gateshead.

(David Rodgers)
Pentax SP1000   55mm Takumar
Kodachrome II   1/250, f2.8

The Southern Region ran down its Bullied Pacifics rather too quickly during 1966/67 in anticipation of electrifying the Bournemouth line, and Eastleigh was forced to borrow six Brush Type 4s from Cardiff to help out until the electric units arrived — the first and only time that the Region has had an allocation of the type. D1921-6 were thus a common but unwelcome sight at Waterloo, and here D1924 heads a typically mixed rake of Southern green, blue and grey, and maroon Mark 1 stock through the New Forest at Beaulieu Road in May 1967 on a Waterloo-Weymouth service. Recent eth conversions have cast the former D1921-6 far and wide, while the loco pictured, later 47247, is now 47655 based at Gateshead. *(Barrie Walker)*
Leica M2   Kodachrome II

An interesting contrast to the many published contemporary views of Scarborough, this July 1966 shot shows considerably more semaphores on that famous gantry. D1864 overtakes another Brush Type 4 to bring in a Sheffield service formed of Stanier stock. The loco's bodysides are oil/coolant-stained, but even then the two-tone green livery still looks very smart, perfectly matched by the small yellow front end warning panel that was incorporated in the design from new. D1864 was a Tinsley loco at the time, and did not stray far until Crewe took responsibility in October 1973. As 47214 and allocated to Carlisle, it was a rare bird at the end of 1986 in still having an operational steam-heat boiler.
(Barrie Walker)
Leica M2   Kodachrome II

Left: The one and only D1733, the first of the type to bear blue livery: Cardiff's flagship was painted like this from new in June 1964 to go on exhibition with the new-look XP64 blue and grey coaching stock. By today's standards, its appearance is appallingly dull. Perhaps the red cabside panels bearing the new "barbed wire" BR logo borne in publicity shots should have been carried in traffic. D1733 itself has not had the most startling of careers, but it has survived two severe front end smashes. As 47141 and later 47614 on Eastfield's books, it has been nominated twice for nameplates but still ran without any at the end of 1986. In 1985 it was repainted in large logo style. The picture shows it south of Admaston, near Leamington Spa on the very last 1110 Paddington-Birkenhead through service on 5 March 1967. *(Michael Mensing)*
Nikkorex   50mm Nikkor
Agfa CT18   1/500, f3.2

Above: The Great Western main line between Paddington and Birmingham was inevitably drastically downgraded when electrically-hauled services started running from Euston in 1966, removing forever from Leamington Spa trains like this, an absolutely brand-new Landore-based D1753 on the up "Birmingham Pullman". The 47s had taken over from steam two years earlier, and are still seen in large numbers on the route. This loco had migrated to the Eastern Region when renumbered 47160 in 1974, and after a spell north of the border entered Crewe Works for conversion to 47605 and yet another home, Stratford. *(Bryan Hicks)*
Agfa Silette   45mm
Agfa CT18   1/125, f8

Above: The last few two-tone green Class 47s 47356/65/6/7/9 were all overhauled and repainted blue at Crewe in the autumn of 1977, and not before time judging by this view of an exceedingly scruffy 47369 at Toton depot on 2 July, a few days before it was called to Crewe. It was built as D1888 for Tinsley in July 1965, but spent most of its career in Nottinghamshire and was transferred to Crewe diesel depot in January 1985. *(Howard Johnston)*
Praktica LB2   Ektachrome 64

Right: A train was chartered from Spalding to King's Cross on 5 March 1970 to deliver a petition to the House of Commons to protest against the closure of the East Lincolnshire route from Grimsby. The headboard honours the organiser, local councillor Charlie Peck, but the train was poorly patronised. Far worse, the line closed the following October. Today, only the Spalding-Peterborough section remains open. Loco No 1570 is in the transitional livery of two-tone green with full yellow ends and later-style number transfers on the cabsides. The first of the 1964 series allocated to Leeds Holbeck, its many travels since have included Stratford (where as 47017 a grey roof was applied), and Scotland at the end of 1982. *(Howard Johnston)*
Boots Beirette   49mm Meritar
Ektachrome X   1/125, f8

Right: The first repaints in blue livery carried more elaborate embellishments than of late, notably BR barbed wire logos and numbers at both ends. There is also no doubting the 47s looked better when the headcode panel was in operation. D1932, a mere three-year-old Bristol Bath Road loco when pictured at Crewe North depot on 18 May 1969, is featured elsewhere in this book as push-pull No 47701. *(Norman Preedy)*
Voigtlander Vito B   Agfa CT18   1/125, f8

Left: Thank goodness BR never chose pink livery for its loco fleet! Collision damage sustained at Peterborough by 47046 (late D1628) on 29 September 1974 was seen as the ideal opportunity to equip the repaired bodyshell at Crewe Works as a testbed for the new GEC/Ruston Paxman 3250hp engine soon to go into the 56s. Renumbered 47601, it is seen here in works undercoat on 1 April 1976. (See also p35.) *(Bob Casselden)*
Praktica   Agfa CT18   1/125, f5.6-8

The penultimate Class 47 returns home to Loughborough. D1960 did not emerge from the Brush Falcon Works until July 1967 (but D1961 took nearly another year), and stayed a Midland loco as 47514 until converted to push-pull and sent to Scotland in 1979 as 47703 *Saint Mungo*. The 0000 headcode on a loaded passenger train dates this view of 47514 very well as the policy of on-train description has been officially abandoned. The 47 is on a Nottingham-St Pancras service on 29 May 1978. *(Gavin Morrison)*
Pentax SP1000   Kodachrome 25

Diverted from the West Coast Main Line because of weekend engineering work, 47487 hauls powerless Class 86 electric loco 86222 and its train past Brereton Junction box at Rugeley, Staffordshire. The location is only a short distance from Colwich, where two Class 86s were destroyed in a horrific collision between two electric expresses in 1986. 47487 is featured in more spectacular style again on p58. *(Hugh Ballantyne)*
Leica M3   50mm Summicron
Kodachrome 25   1/250, f3.5

Above: The Official Secrets Act prevents us from describing the precise details of what goes on at this location! Vickers Gun Range Box is a remote Furness Railway structure on the Cumbrian Coast between Ravenglass and Bootle and serves the Ministry of Defence branch to Eskmeals, whose own passenger station closed in August 1959. Merry-go-round coal trains from the collieries at Maryport and Whitehaven to Fiddlers Ferry power station are the route's principal freight,

and this unidentified 47/3 is seen on just such a working on 12 August 1982. *(David Rodgers)*
Pentax SP1000   55mm Takumar
Kodachrome 25   1/250, f3.5

Right: The veteran china clay "hood" wagons in Cornwall were in 1986 in the process of replacement by the first new BR-owned wagons for years. Before the change, East-

field's 47108 was well away from its usual haunts on 7 June 1985 along the estuary of the River Fowey near Golant with clay empties from Carne Point to Lostwithiel. The loco, which started life as D1696 allocated to Derby in December 1963, has worked from many locations, and by the end of 1986 moved to the Eastern for the first time, based at Stratford. *(Hugh Dady)*
Nikkormat FT2   50mm Nikkor
Kodachrome 64   1/500, f4

Below: Another Stratford special for a royal occasion involved 47583 *County of Hertfordshire*. The depot emulated its 1977 performance four years later with a striking gesture for the wedding of Prince Charles and Lady Diana Spencer. The white horizontal bands of the large BR barbed wire bodyside emblem were extended to the rear of both cabs, and patriotic stripes inserted as well. The loco, seen at Stratford station on 17 August 1981 with the 1428 Norwich-Liverpool Street service, ran in this style until next called into Crewe Works for the re-application of boring all-over blue. By late 1986 however, this favoured machine was in Network SouthEast livery. It started life as D1767 back in October 1964, allocated to Tinsley, and received its nameplates in a ceremony at Hertford East station on 26 July 1979. *(Bob Casselden)*
Nikkormat FT3   Agfa CT18   1/250, f5.6

Above: Still to be rivalled for its spectacular impact is what Stratford depot did for the Queen's Silver Jubilee in 1977 — what could be more patriotic than giant-sized Union Jack flags on the bodysides of a pair of locos, even if it did take a couple of attempts to get the proportions precisely correct. This is 47164 at Liverpool Street with the 0830 service to Norwich on 9 June, the second day of a week-long use of this "The Jubilee" headboard with two more flags for good measure. New as D1758, the first of a fresh batch to Tinsley in 1964, 47571 is now attached to the LMR. Sister celebration loco 47163 (new as D1763, now 47610) was severely damaged in a collision with electric loco 83004 at Kensal Green in December 1977 and spent almost a year at Crewe under repair. *(Maurice Orme)*
Boots Beirette   45mm Meritar   Agfa CT18

Even if it could not redecorate every loco at its whim, Stratford could still make it stand out in a crowd by its grey roof, bending the rules in such a tasteful way that the authorities were happy to turn a blind eye, and other depots were prompted to respond with their own variations. This is Stratford's 47574 (with black headcode panels restored) in the Great Eastern heartland of Norwich Thorpe station, now utterly altered by advancing electrification. The headboard proclaims the service as "The East Anglian", the 0800 to Liverpool Street, which has previously arrived from Great Yarmouth. On the left 40097 creeps in with Polybulks. Never anything but an Eastern loco since delivery to Tinsley in 1964 as D1769, 47574 was honoured with the name *Lloyd's List 250th Anniversary* on 11 December 1984. Date of this shot is 30 July 1982.

(Ken Harris)
Pentax SP1000   55mm Takumar
Kodachrome 64   1/500, f4

Sunset on the Southern. Raynes Park is eight miles out of Waterloo, and junction for the Epsom line and Chessington branch. The autumn sun is fading fast as 47555 *The Commonwealth Spirit*, an unusual choice of motive power, rattles through with the 1710 Waterloo-Exeter on 20 October 1985. This 1964 Western Region loco was converted from D1717/47126, and received its curious name at St Pancras in April 1979 to mark the return of a Commonwealth expedition across India that year. *(G T Bird)*
Canon AE1   Tamron 135mm
Kodachrome 64   1/500, f4-5.6

The perfect end to a hot summer's evening. The location is Tweedmouth, and the time is 8.00 pm on 10 July 1978 as 47518 speeds through with the up afternoon Aberdeen-Doncaster. We wonder how often East Coast services muster this length of train nowadays. In the mid-1980s' absence of any other type of express power, the 95mph Class 47s hold complete sway of all loco-hauled passenger services in this area — and this loco has plied the route for over two decades. It was built as D1101, a somewhat illogical number considering there were only 12 more 47s to build when the D1500-1999 number series became full up. *(Gavin Morrison)*
Pentax SP1000   Kodachrome 64

Left: Recent passenger specials have lifted the LNWR Amlwch branch in mid-Anglesey from virtual total obscurity, although the line from Gaerwen Junction lost regular passenger traffic as long ago as December 1964. Still healthy however is the daily freight traffic to the Associated Octel fuel additives plant. Motive power was traditionally Class 25 or 40 until the LM ran out of them, and by mid-1985 Class 47s had taken over. On 18 April 1985, 47128 was in charge, coasting through Llanerchymedd. It was soon to enter works for eth conversion and addition of long-range fuel tanks as 47656. It started life as D1719, allocated to Cardiff. *(Paul D Shannon)*
Olympus OM1 200mm Zuiko Kodachrome 64

Above: It is late autumn as 47362 sweeps through Miskin near Llantrisant with a train of steel coil from Port Talbot to Ebbw Vale tin plate works. The loco was based at Cardiff Canton, but within months had returned to the Eastern Region where it was new as D1881 in June 1965. This uninspiring livery of masses of blue and little else has since been replaced by a more stylish (when clean) Railfreight grey. Date of photo, 13 November 1984. *(Geoff Cann)*
Pentax MX Kodachrome 64 1/500, f4

HSTs are OK when they work, but even one power car shutting down ruins any chance of keeping to the 125mph timetable. If both are out of action, there is no alternative but to hook up the drawbar to a conventional loco. Add together the time taken to find a loco, send it to the rescue, and then a 95mph journey, and you can understand the operating staff's nightmare. On 10 February 1985, 47279 (D1981, new to Gateshead in December 1985) tows an errant HST through the snow at Didcot. *(Mike Robinson)*
Pentax ME Super   Fujichrome R100
1/500, f5.6

This is *Fair Rosamund* (the Second). The policy of naming locomotives was largely devalued with the trend from the end of 1984 of virtually indiscriminate switching of plates between locos (and even classes) upon inter-regional transfer, equipment change, or move between passenger and freight sectors. One of the very first locos to benefit with recognition was Old Oak Common's 47618, seen here on the 1030 Exeter-Paddington at North Somerset Junction, Bristol on 10 February 1985, after the original 47510 *Fair Rosamund* was converted to push-pull operation as 47713, moved to Scotland, and was renamed *Tayside Region*. The loco pictured has hitherto managed to stay on the Western Region since delivery to Landore in August 1964 as D1609, and carried an interim number of 47030. *(Geoff Cann)*
Pentax MX   Kodachrome 64   1/500, f5.6

Left: The sun hides the fact that this shot on the 1 in 125 uphill gradient near Standege Tunnel on the Trans-Pennine route was taken on a bitterly cold winter's day. 47442 is in charge of the 1155 Liverpool-Newcastle on 8 December 1981. As D1558, this now generally anonymous locomotive was one of the first to be repainted from two-tone green livery to all-over blue after overhaul in early 1969. Built for the Eastern Region, it has been part of the Crewe stable since December 1972 and has recently been noticeable by carrying cabside instead of bodyside numbers. *(Robin Lush)*
Nikon FM   85mm Nikkor
Kodachrome 64   1/250, f4

Above: Reduced from its glory as a crossing point for the Midland and the Great Western to little more than a passing loop, that's Evesham in the 1980s. At least some "main line" services survive however, and this was 47572 on a diverted Liverpool-Poole working on 6 April 1985. This loco was formerly D1763 and 47168. *(Bob Osborne)*
Canon AE1   Kodachrome 64   1/250, f5.6

Left: A short-lived coaching stock paint style — many say thank goodness — was the red and blue adopted by Sealink for a rake of Mark 1s kept specially for the Stranraer line until withdrawn in the autumn of 1986. On 29 May 1985, they were in the charge of Crewe depot's 47449 on the long single track section near the site of New Luce station, minutes from the end of its journey with the 0857 service from Glasgow. Built at Crewe as D1566 in 1964 for the Eastern Region, this loco was transferred to the LMR between 1971-73 as part of a major motive power reshuffle.
(Rodney Lissenden)
Pentax 6 × 7   150mm Takumar
Ektachrome 100   1/500, f5.6

Right: An original series Brush Type 4, 21 years on. A rake of exhibition stock painted all-over blue for a British Telecom touring display forms an odd-looking train for old D1501, now 47402 *Gateshead,* to take over Copy Pit summit on 24 June 1985 (the witches' haven of Pendle Hill is in the background), destination Huddersfield. The second of the vast class to be constructed at Loughborough in 1962 this loco ran nameless until November 1981. It came within a whisker of the scrapyard at the end of 1986, withdrawn on 1 October but re-instated a few days later as a replacement for crash victim 47464 which was condemned instead.
(Stephen Willetts)
Mamiya 645   80mm Sekor
Fujichrome 100   1/1000

Left: Summer near Dainton Summit on the West of England Main Line, where the 1 in 36 gradient, the steepest of any main line in Britain, should not pose too much of a threat for what appears to be a well-maintained 47567 *Red Star* on the 1427 Paddington-Penzance. This was one of many Class 47s adorned with nameplates as part of the GW150 celebration year, and is particularly distinctive in sporting a large red aluminium star on its bodysides. The loco, D1625 of 1964, was one of a small batch allocated new to Derby, became 47044 in 1973, and was converted to eth operation seven years later. *(John S Whiteley)*
Olympus OM1   Kodachrome 64

Above: Although it was distinctly lacking in pedigree, loco 47500 was adopted as the Western Region's flagship in 1979. At the suggestion of Old Oak Common depot staff, a batch of six passenger machines adopted traditional GWR names, and 47500 was duly christened *Great Western*. Built by Brush in June 1966, it was D1943 on the Midland Region before heading south during 1973. This picture shows it at Didcot on a VSOE special to mark the Post Office issue of stamps commemorating 150 years of famous trains on 22 January 1985, just before the most exciting stage of its career was to begin — see pp46/47. *(Rodney Lissenden)*
Pentax 6 × 7   105mm Takumar
Ektachrome 100   1/500, f5.6

No 47503 thankfully never ran like this in traffic — a rare view of a non-standard paint livery at Chester with the Crewe Works test train on 20 September 1985. The ambitiously large but pleasing bodyside logo was retained as the new standard, but the number transfers were trebled in size. One of the last to be constructed (D1946, July 1966), the loco was new to Toton and has worked variously from Crewe, Bescot and Carlisle since then. (*David Rapson*)
Canon AE1   Kodachrome 64
1/250, f5.6

One of the last of the original D1500-19 series to be granted classified works overhauls before withdrawals got underway in earnest was 47407 (D1506), easily distinguishable from its sisters by black cab window surrounds after its naming *Aycliffe* at Newton Aycliffe on the Bishop Auckland branch on 9 November 1984. Delivered to Finsbury Park in January 1963 with eth and steam-heat boiler from new, it was later exiled to less onerous East Lincolnshire duties until electric-heat stock took over the East Coast Main Line in 1969. 47407 migrated to its current Gateshead home in 1979, and is now seen practically anywhere but East Anglia. This view is of *Aycliffe* at the buffer stops at Liverpool Lime Street with the 1M73 1545 service from Newcastle on 11 March 1985. (*David Stacey*)
Pentax KX   Kodachrome 25

This was Class 48. Five of the late 1965 Brush production series, D1702-6, were selected for fitting with French-built 2650hp Sulzer power units, but the project was abandoned after only five years. The quintet were inevitably kept together, working first from Tinsley, and then Norwich and Stratford depots. Despite subsequent standardisation, they were only eventually split up in May 1983 when this loco, D1706 (now 47118) was transferred from Stratford to Inverness. It also acquired a new-image depot repaint which is non-standard for a Class 47/0. Here it is approaching Crewe with the 3V20 Manchester-Bristol parcels on 12 September 1986. (James F Mair)
Fujica ST705W   Tamron 35-70mm
Kodachrome 64   1/250, f8

There's always one that breaks the rules. The story goes that Inverness depot had only half finished their 1985 repaint job on 47604 when it was needed for service. True or not, 47604 is distinctly non-standard with its wrap-round yellow cabs but little else changed. It is seen at Perth on the 1050 Inverness-Birmingham on 14 March 1986. Formerly D1972 and 47271, this loco has spent almost its entire career based on the Scottish Region. (John Chalcraft)
Mamiya 645   80mm Sekor
Agfa R100S

This is a real face in a crowd, non-boilered 47373 with experimental flashing light on its cab roof for better visibility in Yorkshire collieries while on merry-go-round coal traffic — and on the Southern Region to boot. Although no 47s need to be allocated to the Southern, they are increasing visitors — to Dover, Brighton and Poole from the northern cities, and to many parts of the Region on a variety of freights. This view of 47373 on Whatley-Totton ARC PGAs shows it leaving the Chandlers Ford line at Eastleigh on 6 August 1986. Displaced by Class 56s from most coal duties, 47373 has nevertheless been based in the Sheffield/Leeds area since new as D1892 in August 1965. *(Ken Harris)*
Yashica TL Electro X   80mm Zeiss
Kodachrome 25   1/250, f4

After the Paxman power unit appraisal was complete, loco 47601 (p30) was rebuilt again in 1979 with a 3300hp Ruston Paxman engine to gain experience for the Class 58. By now far and away the most powerful member of the Class 47 fleet, 47901 is also the least travelled, and a lack of trained crews means it rarely strays from the Bristol/Westbury area. Still to be equipped with a front-end high-intensity headlight, 47901 was photographed at Frome on 31 May 1985 on the 1003 Merehead Quarry-Eastleigh stone train. *(Mike Miller)*

Mamiya 645   80mm Sekor
Agfa 100RS   1/450, f5.6

1986 marked the last full year of semaphore signals at the Highland capital of Inverness, and the skyline-dominating gantry will be sadly missed by photographers. Inverness has customised most of its eth 47s with a full depot repaint and the addition of a Highland stag transfer below the driver's cabside window — most noticeable when they stray to Penzance! It's 17 April 1986, and 47546 *Aviemore Centre* still carries its winter snowploughs. The train is the 1230 to Glasgow Queen Street. 47546 was originally D1747 (and also 47154), allocated new in July 1964 to Old Oak Common. It has also spent several years on the Midland, and three years at York before settling in Scotland at the beginning of 1978.

(Les Nixon)

Pentax 6 × 7 Ektachrome 200

By now a Scottish loco and renumbered to 47141, the blue livery prototype D1733 storms out of Aberdeen on 3 September 1977 with the 0945 service to Glasgow, and again this fine signal gantry has disappeared. When they were not cross-eyed, the white marker dots fitted from 1976 onwards in the redundant headcode panel were pleasant enough, but the later blanket application of yellow paint often was not. This loco is now renumbered again in the eth fleet as 47614. *(Gavin Morrison)*
Pentax SP1000 Kodachrome 25

Left: A fill-in turn for push-pull 47703 *Saint Mungo* on the 1025 Edinburgh portion of the service to Birmingham. The location is Midcalder Junction, and the four coaches will be worked south to Carstairs to join the rest of the service from Glasgow. The livery of the loco and Mark 2 stock dates the picture well to 10 April 1982. 47703 (with copycat Stratford silver roof) is the penultimate Class 47, the same 47514 illustrated on p14. The loco is now in stylish ScotRail livery, and the coaches in similar InterCity. *(Les Nixon)*
Pentax 6 × 7   Ektachrome 200

Right: It's 22 October 1981, and the Scottish farmers have still to plough the fields next to the Glasgow-Edinburgh main line at Gogar as push-pull 47711 *Greyfriars Bobby* propels the 1130 westbound InterCity service. Before the advent of the dignified grey and blue ScotRail domestic house style, two of the then dozen push-pull 47s were painted in this nevertheless smart large-logo livery after an overhaul at Crewe. This one (D1941 of 1966 for the LMR and later 47498 for the Western) made the jump from Laira to Haymarket to help modernise the Scottish domestic service, and was originally intended to carry the name *William Wallace*. This was ditched in 1981 in favour of honouring the Skye Terrier dog which guarded its master's grave for 14 years after his death.
(Bob Osborne)
Canon AE1   Kodachrome 64

Above: When the complex InterCity livery could not be justified, a lower-cost repaint with the large bodyside logo and wrap-round yellow ends was adopted as standard for Crewe overhauls from the early part of 1985. Such was the case with 47455, one of the first to be treated, and seen here on the 1710 Swansea-Milford Haven service train containing postal vans at Ferryside, west of Kidwelly, on 5 June 1986.

47455, one of the Crewe contingent for many years, started life as D1575 based at Gateshead. *(Hugh Dady)*
Nikkormat FT2 85mm Nikkor
Kodachrome 64 1/500, f4

Right: No apologies for including old D1733 again, and this April 1986 view of it as 47614 on the Aberdeen-Glasgow postal serves to demonstrate how the loco has changed in the 22 years since it was new. Tell-tale sign of a replacement cab is the lack of recess for the headcode panel, and the livery is the latest large logo style applied en masse at Scottish depots from 1984 and later adopted as standard for passenger diesel locos undergoing overhaul at Crewe. *(Les Nixon)*
Pentax 6 × 7 Ektachrome 200

Locomotive naming, 1980s style. Almost every opportunity was taken to mark an anniversary, service improvement, new station or reward a loyal freight customer with a ceremony. Class 47s inevitably took the brunt of the somewhat transparent glory, although freshly ex-works after eth conversion 47645 did better than most at Blaenau Ffestiniog station on 1 May 1986 when it took a four-coach rake full of invited guests down the branch from Llandudno Junction to be named *Robert F. Fairlie*, after the designer of double-ended steam locos still running today on the nearby Festiniog Railway. By then a Crewe-based loco, 47645 was built at Crewe Works for delivery to Landore in February 1965 as D1659, and stayed on the WR as 47075 until early 1983.
(Larry Goddard)
Fujica ST705   55mm
Ektachrome 100   1/125, f9.3

"We need our loco back . . ." Whether true or not, Stratford depot's efforts not to let its locos stray far from its sights have become a standing joke amongst train control staff. What did they think about one of their pride and joys straying to North Wales? 47585 *County of Cambridge-* *shire,* as always ultra-smart with large logo livery and black marker light panel restored for decoration, leaves Llandudno with the return leg of a charter from Audley End on 12 June 1986. Until 1987 at least, this loco had always been based on the ER. New to Tinsley as D1779 in October 1964, it migrated to Stratford in May 1978 as 47184 and was named and crested appropriately at Cambridge station on 9 May of the following year. *(Larry Goddard)* *Zeiss AM-1   Tamron 105mm* *Kodachrome 64   1/250, f6.3*

43

Left: An immaculate 47574, red bufferbeams, white pipework *et al*, approaches Bradford Exchange with the royal train carrying HRH Prince Charles on 10 June 1981. Although there is an obvious colour clash between loco and coaches, their collective smartness is a redeeming feature. 47574 was a York loco at the time, but in the September made a move to Stratford where it has since been named *Lloyd's List 250th Anniversary* after the world-renowned insurance concern's publication. The loco started life in 1964 as humble D1769, one of a large number for Tinsley depot, and is one of a handful of 47s whose eth conversion coincidentally involved altering only one digit, from 47174 to 47574. *(John S Whiteley)*
Olympus OM1   Kodachrome 64

Right: The idea of painting four Class 47s in lined Brunswick green during 1985 to mark the 150th anniversary of the Great Western Railway was treated with derision at first, but the finished result was superb. Always a celebrity 47 anyway, 47484 *Isambard Kingdom Brunel* was enhanced with new cast brass nameplates, and was understandably spotless on 31 May 1985, seen here on the Frome avoiding line while conveying HM The Queen to Castle Cary for the Bath and West Show at Shepton Mallet. Built at Crewe in 1965 as D1662, it was named after the great engineer at Bristol Temple Meads station on 20 March 1965, and has stayed on the region ever since. The first WR namer to undergo eth conversion in 1973, its career has been marred by three somewhat severe collisions. *(Mike Miller)*
Mamiya 645   80mm Sekor
Agfa 100RS   1/500, f4.8

Above: The grand plan to repaint the four GWR celebrity Class 47s in green went slightly awry when it was realised that 47079 *G.J. Churchward* was in fact owned by the Railfreight sector and not equipped for passenger operation. The work still went ahead, giving Railfreight a somewhat over-elaborate machine for everyday use, with passengers to be hauled only in the summer months. This picture shows it at Tiverton Junction over-dressed for a china clay train from Cornwall on 9 November 1985, also providing a final glimpse of the soon-to-be-replaced signalbox. 47079, built at Crewe in 1965 as D1664, carried the longer nameplate *George Jackson Churchward* until 1978. *(Ian Gould)*
Pentax 6 × 7 105mm Takumar
Ektachrome 100 1/250, f5.6

Right: A chance encounter that probably gave the photographer one of the best action pictures of his career! Both train engine GW green 47628 *Sir Daniel Gooch* and pilot GW green 47500 *Great Western* were crewed and under power on the 1145 Paddington-Penzance on 23 September 1986, working west for Royal train duty. The immaculately turned-out duo are seen passing Newbury. Crewe-built 47628 was originally D1663/47078 for a lifetime's career on the WR, while 47500 (formerly D1943) was a Midland Region loco until 1973.
(John Turner)
Pentax 6 × 7 105mm Takumar
Fujichrome 100 1/500, f5

Left: A bitterly cold winter's day, and the blue bodyside stripe on 47707 *Holyrood* seems totally in keeping with the other hues of the 1125 Glasgow-Aberdeen service leaving Arbroath. Conversion of another four Class 47s to push-pull operation in 1985 allowed modernisation of Aberdeen services, although in reality there were still not enough of these versatile machines to go round. 47707 itself, an August 1966 Brush product, D1949 for the LM, spent from 1972-79 on the Western as 47506 before being called north for its new role. *(Brian Denton)*
Nikon FM 50mm Nikkor
Ektachrome 100
1/500, f8

Right: The Glasgow-Edinburgh push-pull image of the late-1980s. ScotRail is making maximum capital out of its ability to hold onto its dedicated fleet of Class 47/7s and stock by applying a special version of the InterCity livery complete with pale blue stripe, a link with the Caledonian Railway and the early-BR regional colour. 47701 *Saint Andrew*, with bodyside crest, approaches Greenhill Upper Junction at speed on 18 April 1986. Note how this loco, formerly D1932, has changed its appearance since the all-blue portrait on p13. *(Rodney Lissenden)*
Pentax 6 × 7
150mm Takumar
Ektachrome 100
1/500, f5.6

Spotlessly ex-works in Railfreight livery with the new cantrail orange stripe, 47220 was working for the Civil Engineer at Crewe station on 22 May 1986 with ballast empties for Penmaenmawr. The 47, built as D1870 in June 1965, stayed in the Sheffield area until 1982, and then had a spell in the North East before overhaul, repaint, and a new career based at Bristol. Note a certain famous Class 40 on the left of the picture — the pioneer D200, of course. *(David Rapson)*
Canon AE1   Kodachrome 64
1/250, f6.3

This is how Railfreight sees itself in the late-1980s: purpose-built air-braked wagons hauled by a facelifted locomotive. The traffic on the outward trip was in fact very lucrative rubbish — newly-repainted grey and yellow 47337 approaches Swindon with the 4V04 1230 return empties from Calvert to Bath and Bristol on 9 April 1986. The loco is the former D1818, new in February 1965.
(Barry J Nicolle)
Olympus OM1   50mm Zuiko
Fujichrome 100   1/250, f5.6

Above: Railfreight grey livery is colourful when clean, drab when well-worn. Ex-works 47019, complete with orange upper bodyside safety stripe, works the 4M77 Bathgate-Washwood Heath freight through Stonebridge, Durham on 22 May 1986. This loco started life working from Leeds Holbeck in April 1964 as a boiler-fitted D1573 for King's Cross services, changing to 47019 ten years later. It stayed close to the Eastern Region until 1986, but has most recently been based at Bescot. *(Peter J Robinson)*

Pentax 6 × 7   150mm Takumar
Ektachrome 200   1/500, f6.3-8

Right: There's always one that breaks the rules . . . Thornaby's 47363 *Billingham Enterprise* is unique in carrying Railfreight grey livery but with large white bodyside number transfers reserved now for passenger machines. Very smart nevertheless, it is seen here in Tyne Yard on 23 July 1986 with the Gateshead breakdown train attending to derailed wagons. It was its

ex-works condition that prompted its selection for a naming ceremony on 6 December 1985. Never before one for the headlines, this non-boilered loco has spent all its career dedicated to freight, based at Immingham from July 1965 as D1882, and apart from a couple of short spells at Stratford never far from the North East. It is incidentally one of only three of the 47/3s not fitted with slow-speed control. *(Peter J Robinson)*

Pentax 6 × 7   200mm Takumar
Ektachrome 200   1/250, f8-11

It took Railfreight a long time to make up its mind about a new livery for its 200-strong Class 47 fleet, and it will be well into the 1990s before they are all repainted. In a lull of 47/4 eth conversions, 47050 was outshopped from Crewe Works in early 1985 like this. Later modifications to the paint scheme however included orange cantrail safety stripe to replace the white on 47050, as well as somewhat smaller number transfers on left-hand cabside. It is working hard on the climb to Willesden High Level on 15 August 1986 with the 4E66 0800 Southampton-Ripple Lane Freightliner. The loco was built as D1632, allocated to Crewe, but has spent many years on the Eastern before returning to the LMR at Bescot depot in 1981. *(Hugh Dady)*
Nikkormat FT2   50mm Nikkor
Kodachrome 64   1/500, f4

The late 1980s electrification schemes have forced the hurried application of an orange safety stripe to anything and everything. Thus still-blue 47327 is so adorned as it passes Patchway on 6 June 1986 with the Bristol West Depot-Cardiff Pengam Freightliner. The non-boilered loco has been locally-based since 1980, having been new to the LMR as D1808 in January 1965. *(Mike Miller)*
Mamiya 645   80mm Sekor
Agfa 100RS   1/450, f5.6

Left: Who can argue that change is often not for the better? The Railfreight image of the 1980s is superbly reflected in this over-view depot shot of an ex-works grey 47337 *Herbert Austin* at Peterborough on 21 June 1986. Compare it with the old order 47361 *Wilton Endeavour* coupled up to it, and 47419 at the rear. 47337 was named *Herbert Austin* after the pioneer motor manufacturer at Longbridge on 24 April 1986, making the headlines after 20 years of obscurity as first plain old D1818 to

Toton in February 1965, and another two decades at Central Midlands depots. 47361 bears the Kingfisher trademark of Thornaby depot. *(John Rudd)*
Mamiya 645   80mm Sekor   1/125, f8

Above: The only member of the D1500-19 series to be favoured with InterCity livery before withdrawals began in 1986 was 47406 (D1505) *Railriders,* doubtless because of its affinity with the youngsters' rail club of the

same name. This veteran, which is due to celebrate its silver jubilee in June 1987, pulls out of Clapham Junction 20 minutes late on 14 June 1986 with the 1615 Manchester-Newhaven. As D1505, it would have been far more at home on King's Cross-Newcastle expresses, but despite still being based on the East Coast Main Line at Gateshead, it can now turn up virtually anywhere. *(Hugh Dady)*
Nikkormat FT2   50mm Nikkor
Kodachrome 64   1/250, f3

Below: Trust Stratford to be first with another new livery — its 47487 appeared in a distinctly continental InterCity paintstyle which had hitherto been most prominently applied to High Speed Trains, ac electric locomotives and the 73s intended for Gatwick Express services. It is seen here at London Fields in the Great Eastern suburbs on 20 September 1986, nearing the end of its journey with the 1505 service from King's Lynn. *(Hugh Dady)*
Nikkormat FT2   85mm Nikkor
Kodachrome 64   1/500, f3.5

Right: Old Oak Common began InterCity livery repaints on selected 47s in late 1986. An example, No 47549, just named *Royal Mail,* is seen at West Hampstead with the 1140 St Pancras-Bedford "Flying Postman" VIP train on 26 September 1986. Former Bristol Bath Road loco D1724 travelled the length and breadth of England before returning to Old Oak Common in October 1982. *(Hugh Dady)*
Nikkormat FT2   85mm Nikkor
Kodachrome 64   1/500, f3.8

Left: The early summer's yellow gorse glistens as reliveried 47430 nears Culloden with the 2100 Euston-Inverness sleeper on 27 June 1986. The passengers would be less concerned with the scenery however because the train is an hour and three-quarters late! Some of Scotland's domestic passenger 47s have been appearing in the new livery but with the InterCity bodyside legend replaced by ScotRail. This loco, D1542 of September 1963, which was first based at Tinsley, had a few weeks in East Anglia before settling into a long career on the East Coast Main Line. It later moved on to Inverness. *(John Chalcraft)*
Mamiya 645   80mm Sekor
Agfa R100S

Right: The name *The Queen Mother* virtually guarantees that Inverness's 47541 will always be in good external condition as the pride of the depot's motive power fleet. It has carried InterCity ScotRail livery since May 1986, and is pictured at Ladybank, junction for Dundee and the singled section to Perth. The loco was new to Landore in August 1964. First as D1755, and later steam-heat 47161, it has spent spells on every region except the Southern, and was named personally by Her Majesty at Aberdeen station on 20 October 1982. *(Andrew Fell)*
Pentax SP1000   50mm Takumar
Kodachrome 25   1/1000, f2

Above: It was a warm and celebrated welcome home for two Manchester-Sheffield/Wath EM2 Class 77 Co-Co electrics on 16 July 1986 when 27000/1 were repatriated after 17 years service in the Netherlands. They were returned by rail of course, and here 27000 *Electra*, still in Nederlands Spoorwegen livery as 1502, is seen being towed through the Essex coastal countryside that surrounds the Harwich branch by 47220 (see also p50). The location is Bradfield, and the train the 1345 Parkeston Quay-Whitemoor Speedlink. *(Ian Gould)*
Pentax 6 × 7   105mm Takumar
Ektachrome 100   1/250, f8

Left: The North Wales coast line has long been a popular venue to observe what Crewe Works has been up to. Before the Crompton Class 33s were taken off this route, newly overhauled push-pull ScotRail 47701 *Saint Andrew* pilots 33035 through Bagillt, Clwyd on 19 March 1986 with the 1116 Crewe-Holyhead service. *(David Rapson)*
Canon AE1   Kodachrome 64   1/500, f5.6

Diverted from the West Coast Main Line because of engineering work on 14 September 1986, electric loco 87035 *Robert Burns* needs a tow from a ubiquitous Class 47. The stock being hauled by 47543 is typical of the period — a mixture of Mark 1 and Mark 2 stock in either InterCity "raspberry ripple" or blue and grey liveries. The location, Lostock Hall Junction at Preston, is synonymous with the last rites of steam in 1968, but so much else has changed since, not least the track reductions associated with major loss of traffic. Back to 47543, it was one of the first handful delivered to the Western Region as D1588 back in May 1964, but has wandered far and wide since being released from the domestic fleet in 1975. Before eth conversion, it was also numbered 47023. *(Les Nixon)*

Pentax 6 × 7   Ektachrome 200

47079 (D1664) *George Jackson Churchward*, named Swindon May 1965, renamed *G.J. Churchward* March 1979, since refitted with cast brass plates. *(Gavin Morrison)*

47581 (D1764, 47169), *Great Eastern*. Named London Liverpool Street station 7 March 1979. *(Hugh Dady)*

47715 (D1945, 47502) *Haymarket*. Named Haymarket depot open day 19 August 1986. *(Howard Johnston)*

47574 (D1769, 47174) *Lloyd's List 250th Anniversary*. Non-standard lettering, named London Liverpool Street station 11 December 1984. *(John Rudd)*

47500 (D1943) *Great Western*. Named Old Oak Common 27 February 1979, but aluminium plates later replaced with cast brass type to match green livery. *(Hugh Dady)*

47609 (D1656, 47072) *Fire Fly*. Named Windsor, 24 August 1985 as part of GW150 celebrations. *(Hugh Dady)*